The Budding Builder

Edited by Laura Laxton
Illustrated by Kathi Dery

Acknowledgments

The following individuals contributed ideas and activities to this book:

Amy Melisi, Ann Gudowski, Ann Kelly, Ann Wenger, Barbara Backer, Barbara Saul, Bea Chawla, Charlene Woodham Peace, Cindy Hewitt, Cindy Maloof, Constance Heagerty, Dani Rosentsteel, Helen Doran, Ingelore Mix, Karyn F. Everham, Kathleen Wallace, Lauren Brickner-McDonald, Linda N. Ford, Lisa Chichester, Mary Brehm, MaryAnn Kohl, Nicole Sparks, Robin Works Davis, Sandra Gratias, Sandy Lanes, Sandy Scott, Shirley R. Salach, Sue Myhre, Susan Oldham Hill, Susan Rinas, Suzanne Pearson, Teresa J. Nos, Tina R. Woehler, Virginia Jean Herrod

THE
Budding
BUILDER

EDITED BY LAURA LAXTON

ILLUSTRATIONS BY KATHI DERY

Gryphon House, Inc.
LEWISVILLE, NC

Library of Congress Cataloging-in-Publication Data

The budding builder / edited by Gryphon House ; illustrations by Kathi Dery.

    p. cm.

Includes index.

ISBN 978-0-87659-381-3

1. Architecture—Juvenile literature. 2. Building—Juvenile literature. 3. Creative activities and seat work—Juvenile literature. I. Dery, K. Whelan. II. Gryphon House (Firm)

NA2555.B83 2012

720.28—dc23

2011049309

Bulk Purchase

Gryphon House books are available for special premiums and sales promotions as well as for fund-raising use. Special editions or book excerpts also can be created to specifications. For details, contact the Director of Marketing at Gryphon House.

Disclaimer

Gryphon House, Inc. cannot be held responsible for damage, mishap, or injury incurred during the use of or because of activities in this book. Appropriate and reasonable caution and adult supervision of children involved in activities and corresponding to the age and capability of each child involved, is recommended at all times. Do not leave children unattended at any time. Observe safety and caution at all times.

Contents

To the Parents of Budding Builders

CHAPTER 1: Carefully Laid Plans

CHAPTER 2: Building with Blocks and Other Materials

CHAPTER 3: Beyond Blocks

CHAPTER 4: More Than Buildings

CHAPTER 5: Outdoor Projects

CHAPTER 6: Cardboard Box Construction

To the Parents of Budding Builders

Builders shape our world—literally. They find inspiration all around them and then fashion their ideas into reality using wood, concrete, stone, mud, and more. Help your child find ideas and inspiration in this book, and use these activities as starting points to create whatever he can imagine. Help him realize that he, too, can make his ideas take shape and become real.

The process of building helps your child develop many skills, including planning, estimating, and counting. She will look at commonplace materials and the world around her in new ways. She will feel the thrill of accomplishment that comes with completing a project. Your child will enjoy doing many of the activities independently, but the ideas in this book provide wonderful opportunities to create something with your child. Enjoy the process, and be amazed at what you can create—together.

Chapter 1
Carefully Laid Plans

Blue, Blue Blueprints

Create your own "blueprints," and then use them
any day to re-create your building plans!

What You'll Need

assorted blocks

blue pen, crayon, or marker

clear contact paper

empty cereal box

markers

poster board or thick paper

Books to Enjoy

Building a House
by Byron Barton

Hillel Builds a House
by Shoshana Lepon

A House for Wally and Me
by Gene Stelten

The House that Max Built
by Susanna Hill

The Little House
by Virginia Lee Burton

Mike Mulligan and His Steam Shovel
by Virginia Lee Burton

New Kid on the Block
by Jennifer Moore-Mallinos

What to Do

1. Use your blocks to build a structure on top of the poster board or thick paper.
2. With your blue pen or crayon, trace each block to create a pattern of the first floor of your building. This is a "blueprint."
3. Cover the blueprint with clear contact paper. (You may need adult help with the contact paper.)
4. Make as many blueprints as you want to, and store them in an empty cereal box.
   Hint: Cover the box with construction paper, and label it "My Construction Plans" or "My Building Blueprints."
5. Next time you are wondering what to do, pull out some blueprints, and try to create the structures. For an even greater challenge, use two blueprints together to create one structure.
6. Real builders have to follow patterns, too. Ask an adult to show you a real building blueprint, if possible. Different parts of the blueprint show different workers (plumbers, electricians, and so on) what to do.

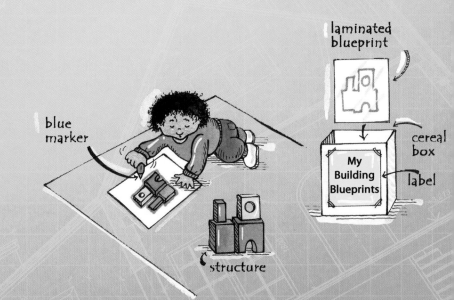

blue marker

laminated blueprint

cereal box

My Building Blueprints

label

structure

Blueprint Books

Make a record of your best block buildings.

What You'll Need

blocks

construction paper, the same color as your blocks

glue

markers

paper

scissors

stapler

Books to Enjoy

The Lot at the End of My Block
by Kevin Lewis

Machines at Work
by Byron Barton

The New Kid on the Block
by Jack Prelutsky

What to Do

1. Trace the different shapes of the blocks on construction paper that matches the color of each block.
2. Cut out the paper block shapes.
3. Create a building using the blocks.
4. Re-create your work by gluing cutouts of the blocks that match the first layer of your building onto a piece of paper, taking care to maintain the same shapes and placement of the blocks. (You may need an adult's help or guidance for this step.)
5. Repeat this process on a new piece of paper for the second layer of blocks in your structure.
6. Continue with a new sheet of paper for each layer of the building. Label the pages with "first floor," "second floor," and so on.
7. Name your creation, and make a cover for the blueprint book. Staple all the pages together.
8. If you have enough blocks, try to re-create the building using only the blueprint book, and compare the structure to the one you built in step 3.

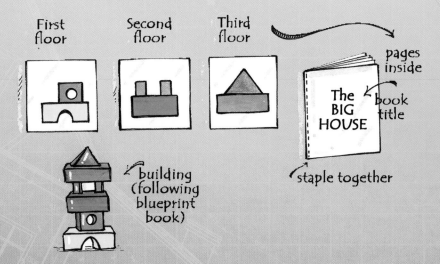

First floor

Second floor

Third floor

pages inside

The BIG HOUSE

book title

staple together

building (following blueprint book)

"Look What I Built"
Photo Album

If a picture is worth a thousand words, then it's a good idea to show off your work!

What You'll Need

camera

marker or pen

paper (or sticky notes)

photo album

Books to Enjoy

The Block Mess Monster
by Betsy Howie

A Photo for Greta
by Anna Alter

What to Do

1. When you create a building or structure that you think is especially wonderful, take a picture of it.
2. Print the photos.
3. Put a copy of each picture in a photo album.
4. Write a caption for each photo on paper or sticky notes, and place the captions under the photos.
5. Include names that you create for your buildings and structures, writing the names in each label. (Ask an adult for help with this step, if you need it.)
6. Keep the album near your blocks or building materials. From time to time, pull it out and look at your past creations.

Where Do You Live?

Plan and build a model of the kind of home you would like to live in.

What You'll Need

construction paper

construction paper rectangles and squares

crayons or markers

empty cereal box

glue

scissors

tape

Books to Enjoy

Home by Jeannie Baker

A House Is a House for Me by Mary Ann Hoberman

My House: A Book in Two Languages by Rebecca Emberley

What to Do

1. Look at or read books about homes.
2. Open a cereal box at its seams, and turn it inside out, with the plain side facing out. Reglue the seams and, if necessary, tape the sides. Allow the seams to dry. (You may need help from an adult with this step.)
3. Think about the different types of homes in which people live, such as apartments, houses, trailers, and boats. Decide to make a home like the one you live in or make a different home.
4. Pick a color you would like the outside of your home to be, and lightly color the box that color.
5. If you decide to make an apartment, you may want to decorate the box vertically. If you make a house, you may want to decorate it horizontally. If you make a trailer, you can add wheels to it.
6. Draw windows and doors or glue cut-out rectangles and squares on the box. Draw other additions on the house, too. As you work, think about the features you chose for your house and why you chose them.
7. Fold a piece of brown construction paper in half vertically to form a roof. Cut it, if necessary, and glue it in place.
8. Write the numbers of your address over the front door.

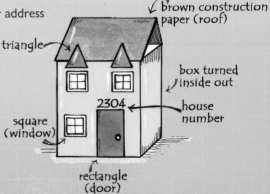

brown construction paper (roof)

triangle

box turned inside out

house number

2304

square (window)

rectangle (door)

Special Delivery: Blocks!

The fun starts even before you begin building, if you extend your imagination to include moving your building materials.

What You'll Need

large wood or plastic trucks

small blocks

Books to Enjoy

1 Is One by Tasha Tudor

Count! by Denise Fleming

One Big Building: A Counting Book About Construction by Michael Dahl

One Gorilla: A Counting Book by Atsuko Morozumi

Ten, Nine, Eight by Molly Bang

What to Do

1. Carry toy trucks and small blocks outside. Use the trucks to move the blocks to where you want to build.

2. Decide what you want to build, where you want to build it (your construction site), and which blocks you need first.

3. Count the blocks you need and then use one of your trucks to deliver the blocks to your construction site.

4. Build with the first load of blocks. You may want to use a set of blueprints you created (page 10) to make your building.

5. On your next trip, put the blocks you need next in the truck, and deliver them to your building site. Count out loud as you load and deliver those blocks.

6. Continue delivering loads of blocks to your construction site until your building is finished!

Chapter 2
Building with Blocks and Other Materials

Build a House

Use boxes and tubes to make your own hideaway!

What You'll Need

boxes in a variety of sizes (shoeboxes, gift boxes, shipping boxes, appliance boxes, and any other box that lends itself to building)

cardboard, bubble wrap, and any other building materials

duct tape

glue

masking tape

paper-towel tubes and wrapping-paper tubes

Books to Enjoy

Building a House by Byron Barton

How a House Is Built by Gail Gibbons

Playhouse by Robert Munsch

What to Do

1. Ask an adult to help you gather a variety of possible building materials that you can use to build a playhouse.

2. Work with a friend or adult, and create a structure. While you build, think about the shape of the structure, how you should construct it, and so on. Even if you don't know if something will work, try it anyway and see what happens.

3. Once you are happy with your playhouse, add animals, cars, or anything else you might want.

4. Play!

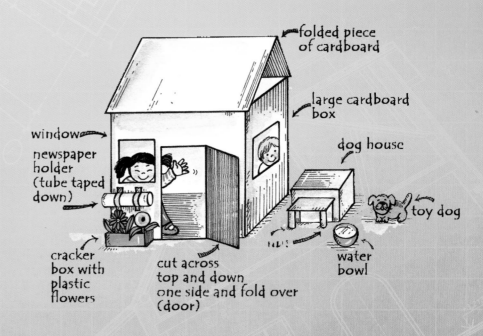

folded piece of cardboard

large cardboard box

dog house

window

toy dog

newspaper holder (tube taped down)

cracker box with plastic flowers

cut across top and down one side and fold over (door)

water bowl

Create a Community

Use paper, markers, and your imagination to create your own personal community inside a shoebox.

What You'll Need

construction paper

glue

markers, crayons

scissors

shoebox

Books to Enjoy

Aesop's Fable, "City Mouse and Country Mouse" (any version)

Going Home by Eve Bunting

I Know a Lady by Charlotte Zolotow

Trashy Town by Andrea Zimmerman and David Clemesha

What to Do

① Find a shoebox. If you would like, decorate the outside. Also, think about what buildings and sites you would like to include in the community that you will create in the shoebox.

② Use construction paper and scissors to cut out buildings, trees, landmarks, and so on. (Ask an adult for help with the scissors, if necessary.) Decorate the buildings and other landmarks with the markers, and think about where each building should go in the box.

③ Fold the bottoms of your cutouts to form a lip. You can then use those to glue the buildings to the inside of the box.

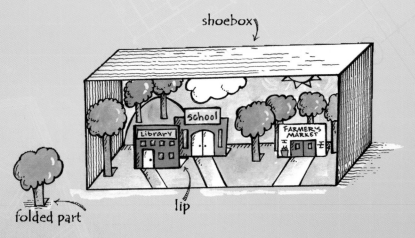

shoebox

folded part

lip

Try These Ideas!

■ Go on a walking tour of your community. Visit places such as the local bakery, police station, fire station, and doctor's office.

■ Make a map of your community or neighborhood. Draw streets, buildings, and parks.

My Town

Create your town using blocks and photos.

What You'll Need

blocks

camera or existing pictures of
town

clear contact paper (optional)

Books to Enjoy

The Fire Station
by Robert Munsch

I Read Signs
by Tana Hoban

Keats's Neighborhood
by Ezra Jack Keats

The Little House
by Virginia Lee Burton

What to Do

1. On a nice afternoon, ask an adult to take you around your town. Take photos of various buildings, structures, or landmarks. You may want to photograph a hospital, grocery store, bank, post office, police station, famous statues, fountains, and so on. As you travel around, talk about each structure and its purpose.

2. Print the photos. With an adult's help, use clear contact paper to attach photos to wooden building blocks. (If you have old blocks that aren't safe to play with because of splintering, this is a great way to reuse them.) You can use tape or glue, but contact paper protects photos best.

3. Use these photo blocks to create your own town, complete with roads. Include as many of the photo blocks as possible. What structures do you think a town needs, and why?

block

photo

block

green paper
(stone path
drawn on)

Lumber Town

To learn to work with wood, ask an adult for permission and help, then find some wood pieces and go to town—your own lumber town, that is!

What You'll Need

magazines

markers

paint and paintbrushes

scissors

scraps of lumber

thick work gloves

wood glue

Books to Enjoy

Night on Neighborhood Street
by Eloise Greenfield

On the Town:
A Community Adventure
by Judith Caseley

Tales of Trotter Street
by Shirley Hughes

What to Do

1. Think about neighborhoods: What are they? Who lives in a neighborhood?
2. With an adult's help, select several scrap pieces of lumber. Look at the shape of the wood, and think about what neighborhood building it reminds you of. It could be a home, grocery store, department store, toy store, library, museum, hospital, or a police or fire department.
3. Construct your buildings, using wood glue to hold your structure together. (You may need adult help with this step.)
4. Let the glue dry undisturbed.
5. Use the paint and markers to decorate each structure so it resembles the building it represents. Decorative windows and doors can be cut out of colorful magazine pages and glued on after the paint dries.
6. Use the new buildings to re-create your neighborhood or to create an entirely new one!

Try This!

Make a neighborhood mat to put the buildings on. On a large, flat piece of cardboard, draw in city streets and rural roads. Add fields, grassy areas, parks, parking lots, and crosswalks at the intersections as appropriate.

Fairy-Tale Cottage

Ask an adult to read your favorite fairy tale to you. Then create a fairy-tale cottage, using frosting instead of magic.

What You'll Need

empty 4½" x 4½" x 5" tissue box

paper cut into a 5" x 1½" piece, any color

plastic resealable sandwich bag

royal frosting (see recipe on page 21)

scissors

small food items, such as lollipops, jelly beans, popcorn, small pretzels, candy canes, and so on

smock or old shirt

stiff paper cut into an 8½" x 6½" piece, any color

tape

What to Do

1. Use the tissue box as the base of your house. Fold the larger piece of paper in half. Open it up, and spread it over the top of the house. Tape it to keep it in place. This is the roof.

2. Mark the smaller piece of paper into five equal sections, then fold it (you may need an adult's help). Open up the paper, and tape the first section on top of the last section, so it looks like a block open at the top and bottom.

3. Cut a V in the front and back of this block, then turn it V-side down, and set it on top of the house as the chimney.

4. Follow the recipe on the next page to make royal frosting. Scrape the frosting into the plastic bag, zip the bag shut, and snip off a little corner of the bag with the scissors.

5. Put on a smock or old shirt, and decorate the fairy-tale "gingerbread" house. Squeeze the sandwich bag so the frosting comes out of the hole in the corner. Now, you can draw designs on the house and use the frosting to glue the small food items on.

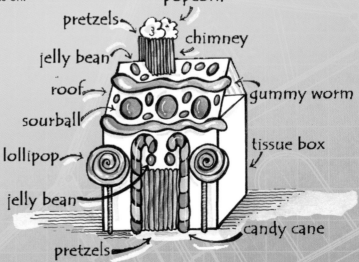

popcorn

pretzels

chimney

jelly bean

roof

gummy worm

sourball

lollipop

tissue box

jelly bean

candy cane

pretzels

Fairy-Tale Cottage

Ask an adult to read your favorite fairy tale to you. Then create a
fairy-tale cottage, using frosting instead of magic.

Books to Enjoy

Castles, Caves, and Honeycombs
by Linda Ashman

Hansel and Gretel
by James Marshall

The House That Drac Built
by Judy Sierra

The Knight and the Dragon
by Tomie dePaola

Over at the Castle
by Boni Ashburn

Princess in the Forest
by Sibylle von Olfers

Royal Frosting Recipe

4 cups confectioner's sugar
2 tablespoons meringue powder
½ to ¾ cup warm water
Equipment: measuring cups and spoons, mixing bowl, spoon, electric mixer

Blend together the sugar and meringue powder in a bowl. Add the water and blend
with an electric mixer on high for about 5 minutes, until stiff peaks form.

Hint: Royal frosting hardens very quickly. Keep it covered with a damp towel until
ready to use.

Try This!

Imagine other possibilities, such as a fairy-tale castle from which you can rule your
world. Use boxes and blocks to create a castle. When the castle is finished, use
crowns, hats, and scarves to act out stories about castles. The stories can be from
books or ones that you make up.

Cardboard Cityscapes

No matter where you live, you can gaze upon a city skyline that you make yourself.

What You'll Need

aluminum foil

cardboard

construction paper

glue

markers, paint, or crayons

pictures of cities and city skylines (in magazines and books, and from the Internet)

scissors

Books to Enjoy

Alphabet City
by Stephen Johnson

City by Numbers
by Stephen Johnson

Richard Scarry's Busy Town
by Richard Scarry

Skyscraper by Susan Goodman
and Michael Dolittle

What to Do

1. Cut cardboard into building shapes, about 4" x 12". Ask an adult to help you cut a variety of roof designs, such as gabled, flat, and so on. Vary the heights of the cardboard buildings by cutting ½", 1", or 1½" from the bases of the buildings. (You may need to ask an adult for help.)

2. Look at pictures of cities and city skylines.

3. Choose several buildings from the cardboard cutouts. Cut the 9" x 12" construction paper into 9" x 3" strips.

4. Trace each building separately on a piece of construction paper, and cut that out.

5. Line up the buildings and glue the 9" x 3" strip of paper to hinge two buildings together, leaving a ¼" space to move the buildings back and forth. Glue another paper hinge on the back and repeat with the last building so that all three are joined. (You probably will need an adult to help you with this step.)

6. To decorate the buildings, glue the paper cutouts on the matching cardboard cutout (covering the hinges). Put heavy books on the buildings as the glue dries to prevent wrinkling.

7. Add doors, windows, shingles, and other architectural features. Glue on aluminum-foil windows, if desired.

8. Stand the building threesomes together on a large flat surface for a big-city look.

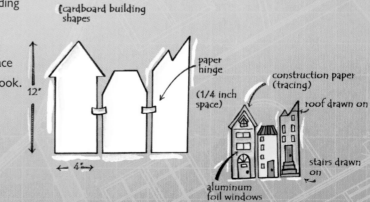

22

Tube Art

Not all structures are made of blocks and boards. For example, your playground jungle gym might be made of tubes. What can you build with wrapping-paper or paper-towel tubes?

What You'll Need

big sheet heavy cardboard or piece of wood for a base

glitter (optional)

lots of glue

newspaper

paint

paintbrushes

paper tubes from paper towels or wrapping paper (as many as you can collect)

scissors (adult use only)

small bowl

Books to Enjoy

Housebuilding for Children by Lester Walker

Kazumura Cave: The World's Longest Lava Tube by Brad Burnham

A Year at a Construction Site by Nicholas Harris

What to Do

1. Cover the table with newspaper for easy cleanup.
2. Place the base and your other materials on the newspaper.
3. Put lots of glue in the small bowl.
4. Ask an adult to cut the tubes to the lengths you want. Or, you may not want to cut them at all!
5. Use a paintbrush to cover a tube entirely with glue.
6. Place the tube on the base anywhere you choose.
7. Repeat steps 5 and 6, building an interesting structure with the tubes. Will you stack them? put them side by side? arrange them in a pattern?
8. Let the structure dry overnight.
9. Paint your structure any way you choose. Let the paint dry.
10. Admire your work!

Try This!

Sprinkle glitter on your structure while the paint is still wet, for a sparkly effect.

Building Bridges

Build two towns, then link them with a bridge you create out of recycled materials.

What You'll Need

blocks

boxes

cardboard scraps

2 chairs

dolls

margarine tubs

masking tape

milk cartons

paper-towel tubes

Styrofoam or paper trays

toy cars

Books to Enjoy

Bridges by Seymour Simon

Bridges Are to Cross
by Philemon Sturges

Pop's Bridge by Eve Bunting

What to Do

1 Set the two chairs about 3' apart, facing each other.

2 Create two towns—one on the seat of each chair—with your dolls, cars, and some boxes or blocks for houses and other buildings.

3 Use your recycled materials to construct a bridge between the two communities. Tape the materials together with masking tape as you build.

4 Pretend that the people in the two towns are crossing the bridge to visit each other.

Velcro and Styrofoam

Recycle pieces of Styrofoam to use again and again as building materials.
Your creations will stick together with Velcro!

What You'll Need

leftover Styrofoam pieces in
varying sizes

peel-and-stick Velcro strips

scissors

Books to Enjoy

Block City
by Robert Louis Stevenson

Mistakes That Worked
by Charlotte Jones

Penguin Comes Home
by Louise Young

What to Do

1. Ask an adult to cut the Velcro strips into various sizes, depending on how big the Styrofoam pieces are.
2. Peel the backing off a Velcro strip, and stick the strip onto the Styrofoam so that the soft side is facing out.
3. Place the hooked side of the strip on another spot on the same piece or on another piece.
4. Continue peeling and sticking the Velcro strips until each Styrofoam piece has a few of both kinds (soft and hooked).
5. Build structures by sticking the soft sides of the Velcro strips to the hooked sides of other strips. Your Styrofoam pieces will stick together!
6. If you change your mind about your creation, just pull the strips apart and move your pieces around. Stick the pieces together in a new combination.

Reprinted with permission from *Block Play* by Sharon MacDonald. Published by Gryphon House, Inc., © 1996.

Chapter 3
Beyond Blocks

Big Bricks

Some Native American tribes used a mud mixture called adobe to make their housing. You, too, can make a house out of common mud.

What You'll Need

cookie sheet

grass

large mixing bowl (that is no longer used for preparing food)

large spoon

loaf pan (that is no longer used for baking food)

old shirt or smock

oven

soil

toothpicks

water

Books to Enjoy

Grandmother's Adobe Dollhouse
by MaryLou Smith

If You Lived with the Hopi
by Anne Kamma

Is My Friend at Home?
Pueblo Fireside Tales
by John Bierhorst

This House Is Made of Mud
by Ken Buchanan

What to Do

1. Mix together the soil, grass, and water in the bowl. Add more water, grass, or soil as needed until the mixture is very thick.
2. Touch, squeeze, and mold the mixture for a few minutes, and notice how it feels. Does it feel different from what you expected?
3. Place enough of the mixture into the loaf pan to mold it into the shape of a brick or rectangle.
4. Turn the loaf pan over and tap the bottom to remove the mud mixture. Place it on the cookie sheet (ask an adult for help if you need it). If you want to add detail, use toothpicks to draw windows, doors, or even tiny brick shapes.
5. Bake in the oven on low (250°F) for several hours (ask an adult for permission and help), or bake in the sun for several days.
6. Once the house is completely dry, you can decorate it with construction paper and add accessories such as toys.

Try These Ideas!

- Add more grass and some twigs, and use the mixture to build nests, beaver dams, or caves.
- Make lots of bricks and then use them to make a mud house outdoors. Use the wet mud mixture to hold the bricks together.

paper tree

construction paper roof

baked brick

detail made with a toothpick

play animal

blocks (fence)

Build a Bridge

Instead of cables and steel, toothpicks and craft sticks form the bridge you imagine.

What You'll Need

construction paper

glue

markers

pictures of bridges from books, magazines, or the Internet

Popsicle or craft sticks

string

toothpicks

Books to Enjoy

Bridges by Seymour Simon

Bridges: Amazing Structures to Design, Build & Test by Carol A. Johmann and Elizabeth J. Rieth

Bridges Are to Cross by Philemon Sturges

Richard Scarry's Cars and Trucks and Things That Go by Richard Scarry

Road Builders by B. G. Hennessy

The Three Billy Goats Gruff by Paul Galdone

What to Do

1. Look at pictures of bridges in books, in magazines, or from the Internet.
2. Think about bridges that you would like to build. What two places does the bridge connect? What does it cross over? Is it a walking bridge or a driving bridge? Who might go on it?
3. Use construction paper as a background for your bridge scene, and use markers or crayons to draw the scenery, such as grass, the sky, the ocean, sidewalks, parks, and so on.
4. Build your bridge by gluing Popsicle or craft sticks and toothpicks on the scene.
   Hint: You might lay out the sticks or toothpicks in a pattern before actually gluing.
5. After the glue is dry, draw people, cars, or animals crossing the bridge.

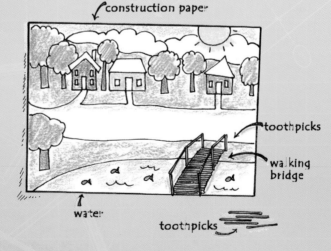

Try This!

Make big bridges on the floor with hollow blocks and unit blocks, then try crossing them with toy cars and trucks.

29

Sand Play

See how high you can build and how deep you can dig in the sand.

What You'll Need

old spoons or plastic sand shovels

sand (at the beach or in a large sandbox)

sand pails or plastic bowls

water

Books to Enjoy

Hamlet and the Magnificent Sandcastle by Brian Lies

Super Sand Castle Saturday by Stuart Murphy

What to Do

1. Challenge a friend or adult to a contest to see who can build the biggest sand castle in a set amount of time (try 10 minutes), or work together to build the biggest sand castle possible in that same amount of time.
2. Next, see who can dig the deepest hole, or work together to dig a deep hole.
3. If you are at the beach, see if you can dig until you hit water. Think about why water seeps into the hole.

old spoon

bucket

shovel

Sand City

Why stop at a sand castle when you can create a whole city? Your imagination is the (city) limit!

What You'll Need

empty, sturdy plastic containers and waxed-paper milk cartons

outdoor sandbox

pebbles, seashells, twigs, acorns, and other natural items

shovels or garden trowels

toy cars, trucks, and so on

Books to Enjoy

At the Beach
by Anne F. Rockwell

Jump into Science: Sand
by Ellen Prager

Ladybug Girl at the Beach
by Jacky Davis

Sand Cake by Frank Asch

Sea, Sand, Me!
by Patricia Hubbell

What to Do

1. Using either pails of water or a hose, wet the sand in your sandbox. Squeeze a clump of sand in your hand, and then open your hand to see if the sand will hold a shape. Add more water until the sand holds a shape but is not soggy.

2. Fill a container with wet sand, then turn it over to unmold the sand. Ask an adult for help as necessary (wet sand can get heavy!).

3. Build a "sand city" with lots of structures. Remember that shells, pebbles, and other objects from nature make fine windows and doors.

4. Create and decorate sand buildings until you have a complete city or neighborhood made of sand.

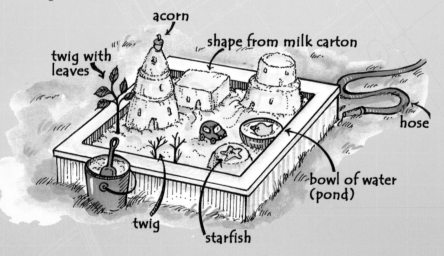

acorn
twig with leaves
shape from milk carton
hose
bowl of water (pond)
twig
starfish

Try This!

For even more fun, bring small cars, trucks, dolls, plastic animals, and other washable items out, and use them to play within the city. Add twigs and moss for trees and grass.

Cube Stackers

Quivering, quaking, wiggling, jiggling buildings provide lots of slippery fun—and a yummy dessert!

What You'll Need

1½ cups of apple juice

baking pan (8" square)

cooking spray

kitchen knife

measuring cup

saucepan

unflavored gelatin

Books to Enjoy

Earthquakes by Ellen Prager

Earthquakes by Franklyn Branley

Jenny Jellyfish: A Tale of Wiggly Jellies by Suzanne Tate

What to Do

1. Wash your hands thoroughly.
2. Ask an adult to boil the apple juice in a pan on the stove.
3. Have the adult stir one package of gelatin into the boiling apple juice until the gelatin is completely dissolved.
4. Spray an 8" square baking pan with nonstick cooking spray.
5. Carefully pour the gelatin into the pan. Put the pan into the refrigerator and refrigerate at least three hours (or overnight).
6. Once the gelatin is set, cut it into cubes, and put the cubes on a plate. This step might be easier with adult help.
7. Wash your hands.
8. Construct interesting sculptures and buildings. Use toothpicks to hold the cubes together, if you need to. Does the texture of the gelatin cubes make it harder or easier to build things than you thought? Which is easier, gelatin cubes or blocks? Which is more stable?
9. Serve your creation to your family as dessert! (Just pull out the toothpicks before you eat.)

Try This!

Add food coloring to the gelatin-and-juice mixture to create colored cubes. Make several colors of cubes to enhance the fun!

Toothpick Sculptures

Create crazy, out-of-this-world structures by sticking Styrofoam pieces together with toothpicks.

What You'll Need

glue

scissors

scraps of construction and wrapping paper

Styrofoam balls, blocks, and packing peanuts

Styrofoam meat trays (washed and dried), cut in pieces

wooden toothpicks

Books to Enjoy

1 to 10 and Back Again: A Getty Museum Counting Book

Building on Nature: The Life of Antoni Gaudi by Rachel Rodriguez

Getting to Know the World's Greatest Artists Series by Mike Venezia

What to Do

1. When looking at books and walking outdoors, pay attention to the many different forms of structures that you see.
2. Ask an adult to show you how to safely connect the Styrofoam pieces with toothpicks. Be careful not to stick your finger!
3. Let your imagination go wild, and create three-dimensional sculptures and structures with the Styrofoam and toothpicks.
4. When you finish, you can decorate the structures and sculptures by gluing paper scraps to them.

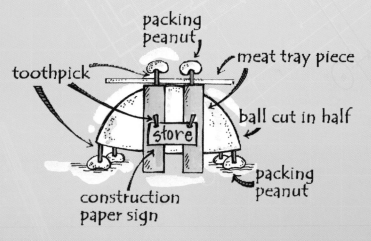

packing peanut

meat tray piece

toothpick

ball cut in half

store

packing peanut

construction paper sign

Try This!

Use neon-colored paper and photocopy pictures of traffic signs with different shapes. Use glue to attach a picture to one end of a toothpick. Stick the other end of the toothpick into a Styrofoam block. Make cars, trucks, and buses from Styrofoam blocks.

Building an Igloo

Can you make a curved building out of blocks? People who build ice igloos do! Try it!

What You'll Need

large pieces of Styrofoam

masking tape

pictures of different types of homes, including igloos

Books to Enjoy

Homes in Many Cultures
by Heather Adamson

Houses and Homes
by Ann Morris

The Polar Bear Son: An Inuit Tale
by Lydia Dabcovich

What to Do

1. Look at pictures of different types of homes that people live in around the world. Compare the houses in hot and cold places. Now find a picture of an igloo, and look at how it is made. Would you like to live in an igloo?

2. Ahead of time, ask an adult to collect large pieces of Styrofoam packing (the kind that is used for shipping) and to cut the pieces into sections to resemble large blocks of ice.

3. Arrange the Styrofoam pieces into the shape of an igloo. Think about how you will get into and out of the igloo once it is built, and leave a doorway. Make the igloo large enough for you to be able to crawl inside and sit.

4. Use masking tape to hold the Styrofoam pieces together.

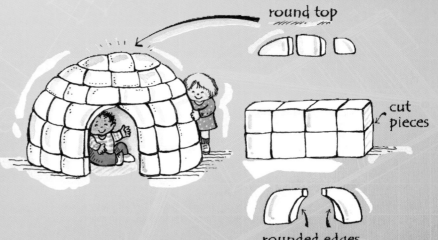

round top

cut pieces

rounded edges (doorway)

Try This!

Use the igloo to provide the basis for dramatic play. What will you use for food? How will you sleep? What kind of clothing will you need?

Ice Castle

What does it take for pieces of ice to stick together? Try this activity to find out!

What You'll Need

freezer

gloves or mittens

ice cube trays and small plastic containers of various sizes

large cookie sheet

large towel

saltshaker with salt

water

What to Do

1. Fill small containers of different sizes with water, and place them in a freezer overnight.
2. Protect your work area with a large towel. Place a large cookie sheet on the towel.
3. Remove the ice from the containers, and place the ice on the large cookie sheet.
4. Look at how the ice froze in the shapes of the containers.
5. Try to build a castle with the ice. You will need gloves or mittens. Do the ice shapes stack the same way blocks do?
6. Sprinkle the ice with a saltshaker. The salt helps the ice pieces stick together. Do you know why this happens? (Salt melts ice, and the melted ice sometimes refreezes, making things stick to the ice.)
7. Can you think of other ways to keep the pieces of ice together? Try a few.

Books to Enjoy

365 Penguins
by Jean-Luc Fromental

Ice by Arthur Geisert

Snow by P. D. Eastman

The Snowy Day
by Ezra Jack Keats

White Snow Bright Snow
by Alvin Tresselt

Slotted Cardboard Construction

Slide them together, slide them apart, let your imagination be your guide!

What You'll Need

dolls, toy furniture, and cars (optional)

large box or tub

slotted cardboard inserts (found in boxes in which breakable items are shipped)

Books to Enjoy

Don't Throw That Away! by Lara Bergen

Grandpa's Corner Store by DyAnne DiSalvo-Ryan

The Three R's: Reduce, Reuse, Recycle by Nuria Roca

What to Do

① Collect a large number of slotted cardboard pieces, and place them in a large box or tub.

Hint: You can also make your own slotted cardboard out of cardboard scraps. (Just let an adult cut the slots for you.)

② When you are ready to build, just slip the cardboard pieces together at the precut slots. (Ask an adult to show you how, if you need to.)

③ If you like, place your dolls or other toys in the buildings you construct.

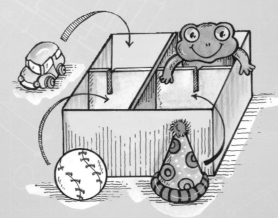 

Reprinted with permission from *Block Play* by Sharon MacDonald. Published by Gryphon House, Inc., © 1996.

Nuts and Bolts Construction

Get down to the basics of building and construction using nuts, bolts, and pegboard to create sculptures and structures.

What You'll Need

nuts and bolts in a
variety of sizes

pegboard

Book to Enjoy

Frankie Works the Night Shift
by Lisa Westberg Peters

What to Do

1. Collect scrap pieces of pegboard. (You also can purchase scrap pegboard at hardware stores for a reasonable price.)

2. Collect (or purchase) matching nuts and bolts. Make sure the bolts will fit through the holes in the pegboard.

3. Create a variety of structures by putting the bolts through pieces of the pegboard and securing them with the nuts.

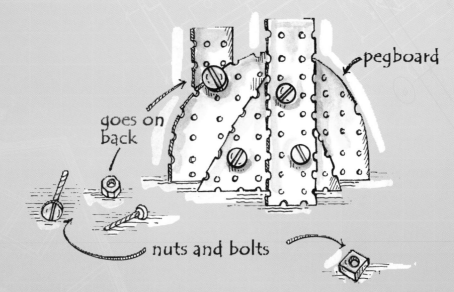

goes on back

pegboard

nuts and bolts

Reprinted with permission from *Block Play* by Sharon MacDonald. Published by Gryphon House, Inc., © 1996.

Chapter 4
More Than Buildings

Paper Creature

As Tall as the Toy

Horizontal Blocks

House Mobile

Who's Caught in the Web?

Marker Organizer

Flower Box Planter

Shoebox Greenhouse

Dominoes

No-Spill Stepstool

Paper Creature

Try building something that is not a building: Use paper to make imaginary creatures!

What You'll Need

masking tape

newspaper

paint

paintbrushes

Books to Enjoy

Bruno Munari's Zoo
by Bruno Munari

Creature ABC
by Andrew Zuckerman

Creatures of Earth, Sea, and Sky
by Georgia Heard

*Strange Creatures:
The Story of Walter Rothschild
and His Museum*
by Lita Judge

What to Do

1. Crumple newspaper to make one body part of a "creature." Repeat for each body part you will need, such as the head, feet, body, tail, and so on.

2. Attach this shape to another crumpled shape using tape. For example, to make a "turtle creature," crumple a large ball of newspaper to make the body, attach a smaller ball for the head, and four more balls of newspaper for the feet. (You might need help from an adult or a friend to do this.)

3. Repeat the process until you finish making a creature.

4. Paint the creature, and let it dry.

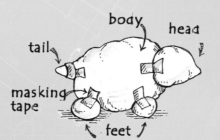

As Tall as the Toy

Architects need to measure and estimate. Practice these skills by comparing the heights of different toys and dolls, and learn how to estimate their heights by using blocks.

What You'll Need

several dolls or stuffed toys, each a different height

uniform rectangular or square blocks, 20–30 of them

Books to Enjoy

How Long or How Wide: A Measuring Guide
by Brian Cleary

Measuring Penny
by Loreen Leedy

One Big Building: A Counting Book About Construction
by Michael Dahl

What to Do

1. Select a doll or stuffed toy.
2. Stand that doll or toy on the floor or on a table. Stack blocks as tall as the doll or toy.
3. If you need to, ask an adult to help you stack the blocks. Together, count how many blocks you need to create a stack that is as tall as the doll or stuffed toy.
4. Repeat the process with other dolls or toys.
5. Look at a doll or toy and, before you begin stacking the blocks, guess how many blocks you will need to make a stack as tall as the doll or toy.

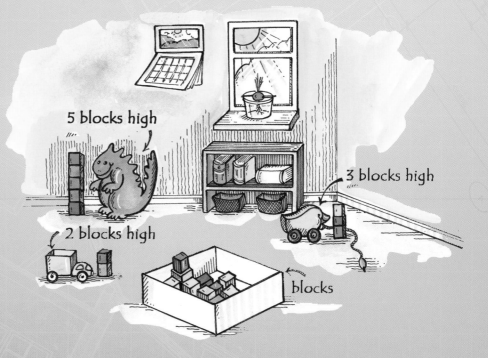

5 blocks high

3 blocks high

2 blocks high

blocks

Horizontal Blocks

Instead of building up toward the sky, use blocks to build structures that
s-t-r-e-e-e-e-t-c-h out on the floor.

What You'll Need

variety of blocks and building materials

Books to Enjoy

Amelia's Road
by Linda Altman

Grasshopper on the Road
by Arnold Lobel

The Wonderful Wizard of Oz
by L. Frank Baum

What to Do

1. You may love to build towers, but towers can only go so high before they fall over. Try building *across* (horizontally) instead of *up* (vertically).

2. How far do you think your blocks can reach? Think about what would happen if you placed them end-to-end along the floor. How far would they go—across the room? If you started building at opposite walls, would the blocks touch in the middle of the room?

3. Build a "road" with the blocks out into a hallway or into another room.

4. Think of other things you can make with blocks in this way. Two ideas are mazes (either for people or play cars) or a paddock for play farm animals.

5. Now create!

Try This!

On a clear, dry day, take the blocks outside. Line your sidewalk or driveway with blocks placed end-to-end.

House Mobile

Instead of a mobile home, this activity shows you how to make a house that's a mobile.

What You'll Need

cardboard

construction paper

hole punch

plastic clothes hanger

scissors

yarn

Books to Enjoy

Alexander Calder and His Magical Mobiles by Jean Lipman

A Day in the Life of a Construction Worker by Heather Adamson

Homes on the Move by Nicola Barber

A House in the Meadow by Shutta Crum

What to Do

1. Draw the different parts of a house on construction paper, such as a chimney, a roof, the house itself, a door, and so on. You will need three or more shapes.
2. Cut out the shapes, and punch a hole in each one.
3. Cut a piece of yarn for each shape, varying the lengths.
4. Thread each piece of yarn through a hole, and then tie a knot in each string to hold the yarn in place. (If you need help with this step, ask an adult.)
5. Use the shortest piece of yarn for the topmost house part (the chimney or roof). Use the next-shortest piece of yarn for the next-highest house part, and so on.
6. Tie the other end of the yarn to the clothes hanger. Hang and see if the pieces form a house. Wait for a breeze, and watch your house fly!

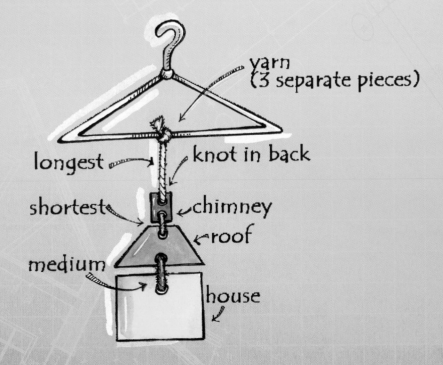

yarn (3 separate pieces)

longest

knot in back

shortest

chimney

roof

medium

house

43

Who's Caught in the Web?

Spiders are builders, too. Webs are carefully constructed traps that spiders use to catch their prey. Experiment with building your own version of a spiderweb.

What You'll Need

4 chairs

picture or drawing of a fly

picture or drawing of a spider

tape

two 10' pieces of sturdy yarn or string or lightweight rope

yardstick

Books to Enjoy

The Itsy Bitsy Spider
by Iza Trapani

Old Black Fly
by Jim Aylesworth

The Very Busy Spider
by Eric Carle

What to Do

1. Place two chairs side by side, approximately 2' apart. (Ask an adult to help you measure and then move the chairs.) The chair backs should face the same direction, toward an open area.

2. Tie one end of each string to each chair back. Tape the picture of the spider to one chair back. Tape the picture of the fly to the other chair back.

3. Approximately 8' away, place the two remaining chairs side by side, about 2' apart. The chair backs should be facing the pictures of the spider and the fly. Tie the two remaining ends of string to these chair backs.

4. Stand between the two strings, very close to the bug pictures. Lightly place your fingers on both strings and face the pictures.

5. Ask an adult or a friend to stand at the other end of the strings and lightly pluck one of the strings. Pay attention to which string is being disturbed, and decide if there is a spider or a fly on the string "web."

6. Take turns playing this game with friends or family members.

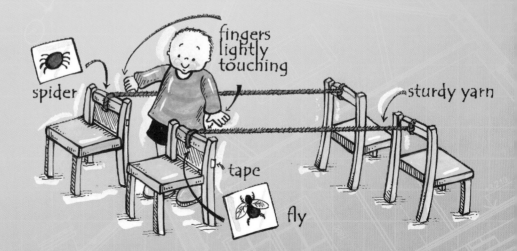

Marker Organizer

Architects use drawing tools to draw building plans. This organizer easily doubles the life of your markers, because they last longer with their caps.

What You'll Need

empty cereal boxes

felt

glue

markers

pen

plaster of Paris

ruler

scissors

water

Books to Enjoy

Adam and the Magic Markers by Isaac Andres

Arnie and the Stolen Markers by Nancy Carlson

Jamaica's Blue Marker by Juanita Havill

What to Do

1. Measure or have an adult measure 3" from the bottom of a cereal box and draw a line around the box at that point.
2. Cut the sides of the box down to the lines.
3. Prepare the plaster of Paris according to the directions on the package. (You may need an adult's help.)
4. Pour the plaster into the box, completely filling it to the 3" mark.
   Hint: Do not pour excess plaster of Paris down the drain.
5. Scrape a ruler across the top of the box to even out the plaster.
6. Allow the plaster to set (check the plaster package for an approximate time).
7. When the plaster is about half-hardened, place the markers—with the caps on and the capped side down—into the plaster. Make sure the marker is straight up. The bottom of the pen cap should be about even with the top of the plaster, and a cereal box should hold about eight markers.
8. When the plaster is dry, remove the cardboard from it.
9. When you take the markers out of the holder, the marker caps stay in the plaster. When you are finished drawing with a color, you can put the marker back into the cap.

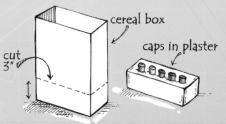

cereal box

cut 3"

caps in plaster

Try This!

Mix dry powdered tempera paint into the wet plaster for added color. Decorate the organizer with contact paper. To prevent scratching the table, glue felt to the bottom of the organizer.

45

Flower Box Planter

Some buildings are for people, but this building is for beautiful flowers! You don't need an outdoor garden to enjoy your favorite flowers. Make a planter, and fill it with beautiful blossoms.

What You'll Need

crayons or markers

flower seeds or small plants

plastic trash bag

potting soil

sand

scissors

shoebox

stickers

tape

Books to Enjoy

City Green
by DyAnne DiSalvo-Ryan

The Curious Garden
by Peter Brown

The Window Box Book
by Karen Fausch

What to Do

1. Decorate the outside of the shoebox any way you choose.
2. Use the trash bag to line the inside of the shoebox. You may need to trim it to fit the box. Ask an adult to help you if you need it. Tape the edges of the bag over the top edge of the box. This will make your shoebox into a waterproof planter.
3. Put a layer of sand about 1" deep in the bottom of your planter. The water will drain into the sand layer and keep the plants' roots from getting soggy. Just don't overwater!
4. Fill the planter with potting soil.
5. Plant your seeds or small plants, and water them (not too much!).
6. Place your planter in a sunny spot, and enjoy your flowers as they grow.

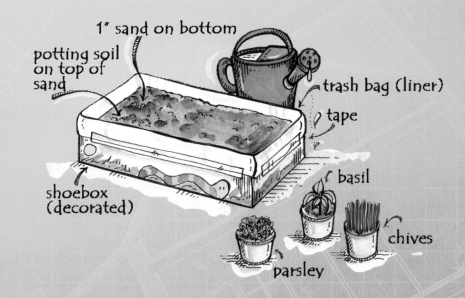

1" sand on bottom

potting soil on top of sand

trash bag (liner)

tape

shoebox (decorated)

basil

chives

parsley

Shoebox Greenhouse

A greenhouse captures light, heat, and moisture to help plants grow. Build a simple greenhouse, and grow plants all year long.

What You'll Need

desk lamp

empty shoebox or small cardboard box

markers, crayons, or paint and paintbrushes

plastic trash bag

plastic wrap

potting soil

seeds (flower or vegetable seeds in packets)

water

Books to Enjoy

The Budding Gardener edited by Mary B. Rein

Green and Growing: A Book About Plants by Susan Blackaby

Out and About at the Greenhouse by Bitsy Kemper

What to Do

1. Decorate the outside of the shoebox any way you choose.
2. Spread 3" or 4" of soil in the bottom of the box.
3. Plant your seeds by making a hole in the soil with your finger, dropping a seed in the hole, and covering the seed with soil.

   Hint: Follow the directions on the seed packet for how deep to plant the seeds, how far apart, and how much light and water to give the seeds so they grow.
4. Water the seeds.
5. Cover the box with plastic wrap.
6. Set the box under a bright bulb or in a sunny spot.
7. When the seedlings have sprouted and are a few inches tall, you can transplant them to a larger planter or to your garden outside in the springtime.

sprouted seedlings

covered with plastic

Try This!

Grow seeds of some of your favorite vegetables. When you have some sprouts, transplant them to a planter or the garden, and grow veggies to enjoy with your family.

47

Dominoes

Have fun learning about cause and effect as you build.

What You'll Need

dominoes

Books to Enjoy

A Box of Red Dominos
by Frances Boricchio

Tumble Bumble
by Felicia Bond

What to Do

1. Stand the dominoes upright in a straight line, about 2" apart.
2. Begin by creating a short, straight line of dominoes. Once you have some practice, create longer lines or curving lines.
3. Push the first block over, and watch what happens!
4. Try again, this time with a different shape. You could put the blocks in a circle or a squiggly line. Experiment with different shapes and structures—which shape or structure works best?
5. For an extra challenge, try this with rectangular blocks instead of dominoes.

Reprinted with permission from *Block Play* by Sharon MacDonald. Published by Gryphon House, Inc., © 1996.

No-Spill Stepstool

Everyone needs a boost now and then, and it's especially rewarding to use a stepstool that you built!

What You'll Need

clear contact paper

glue

magazines

newspapers

scissors

small cardboard box

tape

Books to Enjoy

Growing Like Me
by Anne Rockwell

The Growing Story
by Ruth Krauss

The Growing-Up Feet
by Beverly Cleary

What to Do

1. Find a cardboard box that is the right size and height to use as a stepstool in front of the sink or anywhere you need a little extra height.
2. Fill the box to the top with folded newspapers until it is packed tightly. Overfill it slightly so that when you compress the papers there is a solid feel to the box. Tape the top of the box shut. (This step may be easier with an adult's help.)
3. Cut pictures or large alphabet letters out of the magazines to use to cover the box. If necessary, trim and neaten the edges of the pictures.
4. Glue the pictures or large alphabet letters to all six sides of the box, forming a collage of pictures.
5. Cover the box with clear contact paper to make it waterproof and to preserve the pictures.
6. If the pictures begin to wear after time passes, simply create a new collage on top of the existing one.

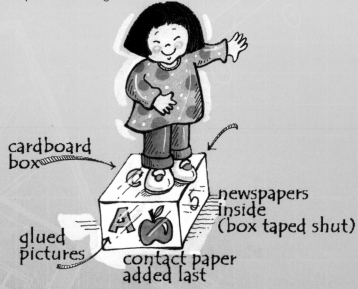

cardboard box

newspapers inside (box taped shut)

glued pictures

contact paper added last

49

Chapter 5
Outdoor Projects

Small Bricks

Stepping Stones

Bird Feeder

Critter Cage

Go Fly a Kite

Let's Go Camping

Small Bricks

This activity shows you how to make bricks that you can then use to build other structures.

What You'll Need

dirt

muffin tins

newspaper

old clothes

plastic bucket

water

Books to Enjoy

From Clay to Bricks
by Stacy Taus-Bolstad

Richard Scarry's Busy Town
by Richard Scarry

"The Three Little Pigs"
by Joseph Jacobs in *Tomie dePaola's Favorite Nursery Tales*

The True Story of the Three Little Pigs
by Jon Scieszka

What to Do

1. Put on some old clothes.
2. Take a plastic bucket outside, and fill it about halfway with dirt. Add water and mix it with the dirt by squishing your hands in it. Use just enough water to form a mud ball. If the mixture is too runny, add more dirt until you get the right consistency.
   Hint: This works best if your dirt has some clay in it. If you have sandy soil in your area, you may need to add some clay to the mixture.
3. Scoop out handfuls of the mud, and then press them into muffin tins.
4. Place the tins or trays in a warm place for about ten days, or bake at 250°F for 30 minutes. If you use the oven, ask an adult for permission and help.
   Hint: If the bricks don't hold together, bake another batch longer.
5. When the bricks have cooled, place newspaper on a flat outside area such as a driveway or deck. Turn the muffin tins over onto the newspaper. You may need to shake or tap the muffin tins to get the bricks out without breaking them. Use the solid bricks for building.
6. Make as many bricks as possible for the most fun in building.
7. Build houses, walls, barns, or any other play structure.
8. Add animals, people, cars, and trees to your play.

Try This!

Add a little plaster of Paris to the mud mixture so it will hold together better. Attach bricks and other items together in a free-form building using plaster of Paris mixed to a runny consistency.

Stepping Stones

Personalize a trail through your yard or garden by using stepping stones you create.
Every step you take will hold a memory!

What You'll Need

damp cloth

9 cups fiber-reinforced ready-mixed concrete

latex gloves

objects to press into concrete

paper towels, if necessary

protective masks

12" round plastic plant drain tray (or saucer) with straight vertical sides

scissors

small tub or bucket

stick or large, old wooden or metal spoon

2 cups water

wax paper

Books to Enjoy

ABCs, Flowers, and Trees
by Janet Lee Harrold

Rabbit's Winter Walk
by Lorna Hussey

The Secret Path
by Nick Butterworth

What to Do

1. Put on the gloves, and put on a mask to protect you from breathing in the concrete dust.

2. Using a stick or old wooden or metal spoon, mix the concrete with 1¾ cups of water in a tub or bucket. Add all the water at once, and stir well to moisten all of the dry powder. If more water is needed, add 1 teaspoon at a time until the mixture has the consistency of thick brownie batter. (Less wet is better.)

3. Cut out a 12" circle from wax paper. Place it into the bottom of the plant drain tray (this will be the mold).

4. Pour the mixture into the mold. Use your hands to press the mixture into the mold. Jiggle the mold from side to side to level the surface.

5. Clean the tools immediately with water—spray from a garden hose works great. **DO NOT RINSE THE RESIDUE DOWN THE SINK.**

6. Make a handprint or footprint in the concrete. Decorate with stones, marbles, or tiles. Make shapes using cookie cutters, or draw letters with a stick.

7. If the stone seems very wet, soak up some of the water by placing a paper towel on the top of the concrete.

8. Put the stone in an undisturbed place for 24 hours.

9. Once the stone is firm, cover it with a damp cloth for a few days to make it stronger. Wait two days before trying to remove the mold, then wait two weeks for it to cure before putting pressure on the stone or putting it outside.
   Hint: This is a great gift for friends, family members, and neighbors!

Bird Feeder

Make a bird feeder to attract our feathered friends to your yard.

What You'll Need

birdseed

plastic gallon jug, washed and dried

scissors or utility knife (adult use only)

twine

Books to Enjoy

About Birds: A Guide for Children by Cathryn Sill

Feathers for Lunch by Lois Ehlert

The Robins in Your Backyard by Nancy Carol Willis

What to Do

1. Cut a section out of two sides of the jug.
2. Tie the twine onto the jug, and tie the jug onto a tree branch.
3. Fill the jug bottom with birdseed.
4. Watch as the birds visit the feeder. Refill the feeder as necessary.

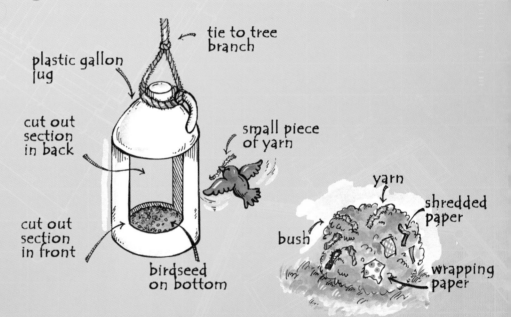

tie to tree branch

plastic gallon jug

cut out section in back

small piece of yarn

cut out section in front

birdseed on bottom

yarn

shredded paper

bush

wrapping paper

Try This!

Select a nice assortment of nesting materials, such as colored wrapping paper scraps, dryer lint, shredded paper, and small pieces of yarn. Place the items on tree branches or in bushes, and watch for signs of birds taking the items to make their nests. Birds are builders, too!

Hint: Early spring is a good time to do this.

Critter Cage

The best way to learn about insects is by observing them. Make a cage that lets you see them up close while letting them have air and light.

What You'll Need

4 chopsticks or other long sticks of equal lengths

hardware cloth; fine mesh screening; or stiff, sheer cloth

glue

masking tape or duct tape

measuring tape

plastic coffee can lids, two of the same size

scissors

tape

Books to Enjoy

The Very Busy Spider by Eric Carle

The Very Hungry Caterpillar by Eric Carle

The Very Quiet Cricket: A Multi-Sensory Book by Eric Carle

What to Do

1. Measure the circumference of the lid. (You may need an adult to help.)

2. Use the scissors to cut a piece of hardware cloth as tall as the chopsticks and as long as the circumference you just measured. Allow an extra inch for overlap.
   Hint: Ask an adult to cover any rough edges with masking tape or duct tape.

3. Glue one stick to one end of your hardware cloth. Glue the other stick about a third of the way down the cloth. Glue the remaining two sticks onto the hardware cloth so all the sticks are the same distance from each other. This will help the cloth stay taut.

4. Let the glue dry.

5. Glue or tape the cloth to a coffee can lid, forming a cylinder. Use the other lid to cover the other end of the cylinder.

6. You have built a "critter cage"! Go outside and look for an interesting insect you would like to observe. Capture it gently, take off the lid, put the insect inside, and close the lid again. Watch the insect for a while, then let it go back into its own world.

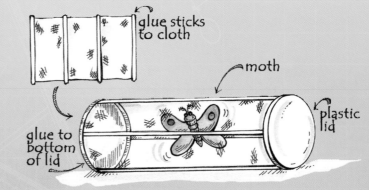

glue sticks to cloth

moth

plastic lid

glue to bottom of lid

Try This!

Using playdough or clay, make bugs. Decorate with sticks, pipe cleaners, or stones.

55

Go Fly a Kite

Build a beautiful kite to play with on a windy day.

What You'll Need

glue

hole punch

hole reinforcements

markers

paper shopping bag, large

ruler

scissors

string or yarn cut in 3' lengths

tissue paper

watercolors and brushes

Books to Enjoy

Abuela by Arthur Dorros

Did You Hear the Wind Sing Your Name? by Sandra De Coteau Orie

Kite Flying by Grace Lin

Windsongs and Rainbows by Albert Burton

What to Do

1. Open up a bag and cut out the bottom.
2. Punch four holes near the opening 2" to 3" apart (two on one side and two on the other side of the opening), and secure the holes with reinforcements.
3. Decorate the bag with paint, markers, or pieces of tissue paper.
4. Attach string or yarn through the holes.
5. Bring the kite outside and run, pulling the kite by the string.

4 holes
reinforcements
bottom cut off
decorated with tissue paper

Let's Go Camping

When we go camping, we build a tent, which is our temporary home. Explore camping from the safety of your own backyard. How do you like it?

What You'll Need

backpack filled with camping items such as a flashlight, canteen, can of baked beans, pots and pans, binoculars, sunscreen, and so on

blanket

heavy books

6' length of rope or twine

old sheet

pillow

two chairs

Books to Enjoy

Bailey Goes Camping
by Kevin Henkes

*S Is for S'mores:
A Camping Alphabet*
by Helen Foster James

When We Go Camping
by Margriet Ruurs

What to Do

1. Have you ever been on a camping trip? If so, what was it like? If you have not been camping before, ask an adult to read you a book about camping.
2. With an adult's permission, pitch a tent outside in your backyard. Choose two chairs that you can tie a rope to. Ladder-back chairs work well, but any two easily moved chairs will do. Set up the two chairs about 5' apart. Ask an adult to help you move the chairs.
3. Tie the rope at the top of the chairs, one end tied to each chair. Move the chairs a bit to make the rope taut.
4. Ask an adult to help you toss the sheet over the rope, one half on one side of the rope, the other half on the other side of the rope.
5. Place a heavy book on the seat of each chair to weigh it down and keep it from tipping.
6. Pull the edges of your tent out a bit, and weigh them down with books or other heavy objects so you have room inside your tent to sit.
7. Stand back and look at your tent. Does it need any adjustment?
8. Fill your tent with a blanket and pillow, books to read, and your backpack of camping items.
9. Pretend you are camping in the great outdoors. Observe the nature all around you: trees, plants, insects, and birds. What do you see?

Try This!

Make trail mix with raisins, dry cereal, granola, chocolate chips, and so on.

Chapter 6
Cardboard Box Construction

Ahoy! Build a Boat

Going on a Train Ride

Jeep Adventure

Space Station

Teepee

Rocket Ship

Working on the Railroad

Creative Castle

Covered Wagon

Puppet Theater

Ahoy! Build a Boat

Set sail to the land of make-believe in a boat you helped make. Be sure you have a place big enough to store the boat, because you can have hours of fun with it!

What You'll Need

chairs

duct tape

glue

large appliance box, such as a refrigerator box

large blue paper

long stick, such as a broomstick

scissors

tempera paints and brushes

utility knife (adults only)

Books to Enjoy

Busy Boats by Tony Mitton

Mouse's Tale by Pamela Johnson

Sailing Off to Sleep by Linda Ashman

What to Do

1. Place a refrigerator box on its back.
2. Adult only: Use a utility knife to cut an opening in the middle of the box in which to place a chair. If the box is too high to step into, cut the box so it is easier to step into.
3. Paint the outside of the box to resemble a boat. Paint a name on your watercraft.
4. Cut out wave shapes from large blue paper, and glue them around the base of the boat.
5. Use duct tape to attach a long stick upright to the back of the boat. Cut out a large triangle from large paper, and tape it to the stick to make a sail.
6. Go sailing!

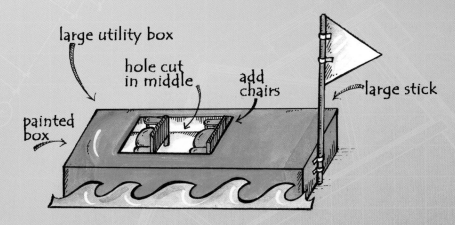

large utility box

hole cut in middle

add chairs

large stick

painted box

Try This!

Pretend you are sailing your boat on the ocean or on a river through a jungle. Add fishing poles, goggles, diving masks, and flippers to the boat, and play!

Going on a Train Ride

Trains used to be the main way for people to travel long distances quickly.
Build a train so you can take your own train trip!

What You'll Need

construction paper

glue and hole punch

large cardboard boxes (big
enough for a child to sit in)

map, atlas, or Amtrak travel
planner

markers

scissors

suitcases and large canvas bags

train props, such as an
engineer's hat, stopwatch, and
a whistle

Books to Enjoy

Chugga-Chugga Choo-Choo
by Kevin Lewis

The Little Engine That Could
by Watty Piper

*Steam, Smoke, and Steel:
Back in Time with Trains*
by Patrick O'Brien

Two Little Trains
by Margaret Wise Brown

What to Do

1. Use the cardboard boxes to design and create a train. Use markers and
   construction paper to decorate the different cars and to make the smokestack
   for the engine car.

2. Plan a trip using the map, an atlas, or an Amtrak travel planner. Cut out tickets
   from construction paper.

3. Pack some items (real or imagined) to take on the trip. Think about what
   you will need when you get to your destination (for example, sunglasses and
   sunscreen if you go to Florida). What will you do when you get there?

4. Pretend to be the train engineer, the conductor, or a passenger. The engineer
   wears an engineer's hat (this can be made out of paper) and rides in the front
   box. The conductor can look at a watch, blow a whistle when it is time to go,
   collect tickets, and use a hole punch to punch each ticket.

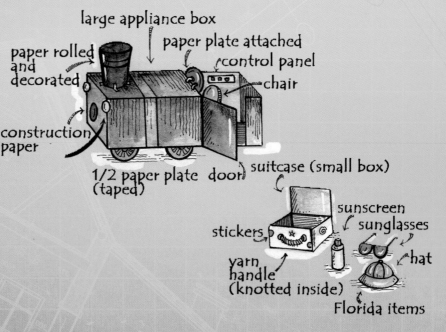

large appliance box

paper plate attached

paper rolled
and
decorated

control panel

chair

construction
paper

1/2 paper plate door
(taped)

suitcase (small box)

stickers

sunscreen

sunglasses

yarn
handle
(knotted inside)

hat

Florida items

61

Jeep Adventure

Build a jeep, and then hop in and take off for an adventure!

What You'll Need

chairs

glue or tape

hole punch

large appliance box, such as a
refrigerator box

long shoestring

paper plates

scissors

tempera paints and brushes

utility knife (adults only)

Books to Enjoy

Sheep in a Jeep
by Nancy Shaw

Starry Safari
by Linda Ashman

Tino Turtle Travels to Kenya
by Carolyn Ahern

Way Far Away on a Wild Safari
by Jan Peck

What to Do

1. Place a refrigerator box on its back.
2. Adult only: Use a utility knife to cut an opening in the middle of the box in which to place chairs. If the box is too high to step into, cut the box so it is easier to step into.
3. Save the part that was cut out of the box. Cut out a circle from this piece of cardboard to make a steering wheel.
4. Paint the outside of the box.
5. Glue paper plates onto the box to make lights and wheels.
6. Place chairs inside the box opening for seats.
7. Punch two holes into the steering wheel circle. Tie it to the jeep using string.

Try This!

Use the jeep to pretend to go on a safari. Use toy walkie-talkies, binoculars, and cameras with your jeep play.

Space Station

Head to the stars, and spend time observing the solar system and galaxies far, far away from your space station.

What You'll Need

black mesh netting

black tempera paint

child-sized furniture

construction paper and crayons

glow-in-the-dark stars and planets

paintbrushes

2 refrigerator boxes

scissors and tape

silver spray paint (adults only)

small magnifiers, penlights, and containers of sand

small pebbles, rocks, or gravel

utility knife (adults only)

Books to Enjoy

How Many Stars in the Sky? by Lenny Hort

The International Space Station by Franklyn Branley

Me and My Place in Space by Joan Sweeney

Owl Moon by Jane Yolen

What to Do

1. Adult only: Use a utility knife to cut along a seam on each of the refrigerator boxes so that they lie flat.
2. Adult only: Cut out two or three small windows and one child-sized door in the sides of the boxes.
3. Paint both sides of the boxes completely black. Allow the boxes to dry.
4. With an adult's help, paint the pebbles, rocks, or gravel with silver spray paint to create moon rocks and meteorites.
5. Tape the boxes together to form one large enclosure. This is the base for the space station. Decorate the outside of the space station with the construction paper and crayons.
6. Tape black mesh securely to the top of the boxes and to the door and window cutouts. This allows the inside of the enclosure to appear dark while allowing for supervision from above and through the windows.

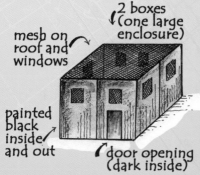

mesh on roof and windows
2 boxes (one large enclosure)
painted black inside and out
door opening (dark inside)

7. Apply glow-in-the-dark stars and planets to a wall inside the space station.
8. Place child-sized furniture inside the space station. Place magnifiers, penlights, moon rocks, and containers of finely ground sand (moon dust) on the table.

moon dust   moon rocks   glow-in-the-dark stars   pen-light

9. Visit the space station! Use the magnifiers to explore the rocks, sand, and the stars on the wall. Use the penlights to read books about outer space.

Teepee

Take a trip back in time, and live like the Plains tribes did.

What You'll Need

duct tape

large box, such as a
refrigerator box

liquid soap

paintbrushes

shallow dishes or plates

tempera paint

utility knife (adults only)

Books to Enjoy

Bringer of the Mystery Dog
by Ann Nolan Clark

Dancing Teepees
by Virginia
Dancing Hawk Sneve

The Great Plains Indians
by Mary Englar

SkySisters
by Jan Bourdeau Waboose

What to Do

1. Adult only: Cut off the top of a large box, and then cut out triangle shapes along the sides of the box (see illustration). Remove the V shapes and corner pieces, leaving the rest.

2. At the top of the box, pull together all the points of the pieces that are left to form a teepee shape. Put tape around them to hold them together. Put tape midway down and at the base. (You will need an adult to help with this step.)

3. Adult only: Cut an opening for the doorway.

4. Paint the box brown.

5. After the brown paint dries, pour different colors of tempera paint into plates, and mix in a little liquid soap. Use these colors to make handprints and other decorations on the sides of the teepee.

6. When the teepee is dry, read books about the lives of the Native Americans who lived on the Great Plains many years ago.

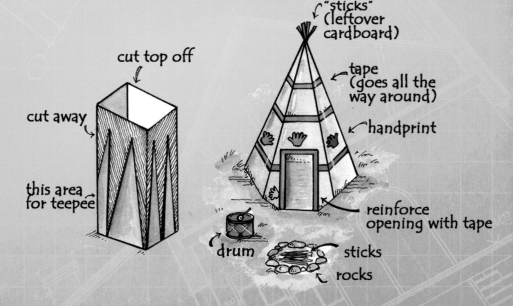

cut top off

cut away

this area
for teepee

"sticks"
(leftover
cardboard)

tape
(goes all the
way around)

handprint

reinforce
opening with tape

drum

sticks

rocks

Rocket Ship

Blast off for exciting adventures in your homemade rocket ship!

What You'll Need

large box, such as a refrigerator box

silver duct tape

small chairs

tempera paint and brushes

two empty wastepaper baskets

utility knife (adults only)

Books to Enjoy

The Best Book of Spaceships
by Ian Graham

Moon Man by Tomi Ungerer

Oliver, the Spaceship, and Me
by Lynn Rowe Reed

Roaring Rockets
by Tony Mitton and
Ant Parker

What to Do

1. Turn the refrigerator box on one side, with both ends closed.
2. Adult only: Cut a door into the side of the box.
3. Turn two wastepaper baskets on their sides, and tape them to one end of the box. These are the "rocket boosters."
4. Put two chairs inside the box for the astronauts to sit on.
5. Use tempera paint to decorate the outside and inside of the spaceship, creating dials and gauges.
6. Take off!

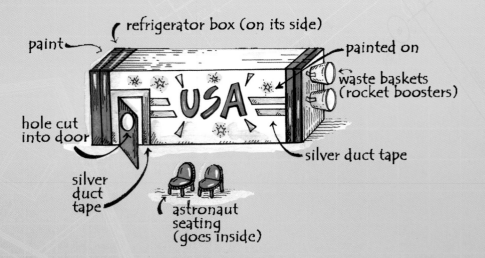

refrigerator box (on its side)

paint

painted on

waste baskets
(rocket boosters)

hole cut
into door

silver duct tape

silver
duct
tape

astronaut
seating
(goes inside)

Working on the Railroad

You may want to spend all the livelong day traveling to distant or imaginary places after you build your personal train.

What You'll Need

black poster board, four sheets

hot glue gun (adults only)

large refrigerator box

railroad play items, such as a conductor's hat, whistle, and so on

small chairs

tempera paint and brushes

utility knife (adults only)

white poster board, one sheet

Books to Enjoy

The Little Engine That Could
by Watty Piper

Railroad John and the Red Rock Run
by Tony Crunk

*Stormy's Hat:
Just Right for a Railroad Man*
by Eric Kimmel

Ten Mile Day and the Building of the Transcontinental Railroad
by Mary Ann Fraser

What to Do

1. Turn the refrigerator box on one side, with one end open and the other closed. The closed end will be the front of the train.
   Hint: The following three steps require a lot of adult help.
2. Cut out a square approximately 12" x 12" from the front end to be the window of the train engine, and two similar squares on the sides.
3. Cut out a large circle, about 36" in diameter, from each of the four pieces of black poster board. Use the hot glue gun to attach these to the large box for the wheels.
4. Cut two lengths of white poster board about 6" wide. Glue each end of a piece to connect the two wheels on each side of the train.
5. Put two chairs inside the train for the engineer and conductor.
6. Use the tempera paint to decorate the outside of the train.
7. Place small chairs behind the engine for the passengers to sit on.

Creative Castle

Build a castle, and rule your kingdom!
Hint: This project needs a lot of space!

What You'll Need

cardstock paper

dowel rods

felt

glitter

glue

large appliance boxes, two

large, round ice cream containers (the bins used in ice cream shops), two

masking tape and duct tape

packing boxes

paint

scissors

sequins

Books to Enjoy

Castles by David Macaulay

The Paper Bag Princess by Robert Munsch

Princess Smartypants by Babette Cole

Snoring Beauty by Bruce Hale

What to Do

1. Use the packing boxes to create a circular wall around an area. Leave an opening for an entryway. Paint the wall if you want. (This takes a lot of paint!)

2. Place the two refrigerator boxes upright so they flank this area. Place one round ice cream container on each refrigerator box. Secure with masking tape.

3. Shape a piece of poster board into a cone and tape it to the top of the ice cream container (you might need an adult's help). Do the same for the other side. You now have two very nice turrets for your castle entry.

4. Cut two large pieces of felt into triangles. These are your pennants (flags); decorate them as you would like. Attach them to dowel rods and slide them down into the openings in the cones at the tops of the turrets. You now have some great castle flags!

5. Use the felt, card stock, sequins, buttons, and yarn to make and decorate castle flags, princess hats, and crowns. You can draw pictures of castle life and create paintings to hang on the castle walls.

Try This!

Make a drawbridge for your entryway. Flatten a large box and draw boards on it with markers or paints. Tape one end of the box to the floor near the turrets. Attach

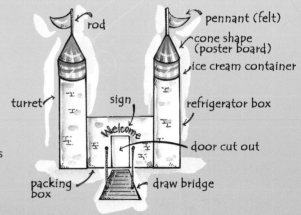

two lengths of rope to the other end of the box. Poke a hole in each refrigerator box and thread the rope through. Tie a knot in the ends of the rope to keep it from coming back through the holes. Raise the drawbridge by pulling on the ropes.

67

Covered Wagon

Westward ho! Saddle up, and head out for adventure!

What You'll Need

brown construction paper

canvas fabric or a large blanket, white or off-white

hobby horse

hula hoops, hollow plastic

large appliance box

markers with large tips

masking or duct tape and rope

old pots and pans

pioneer clothes (bonnets, cowboy hats, old dresses, old dress pants, suspenders, and flannel shirts)

utility knife (adults only)

Wagon Wheels
by Barbara Brenner

Books to Enjoy

Covered Wagon, Bumpy Trails
by Verla Kay

Daily Life in a Covered Wagon
by Paul Erickson

*If You Traveled West
in a Covered Wagon*
by Ellen Levine

The Josefina Story Quilt
by Eleanor Coerr

Three Names
by Patricia MacLachlan

What to Do

1. Read *Wagon Wheels* by Barbara Brenner with an adult. Think about the story. How would you feel if you and your parents moved to a new and strange place? Pioneers built their homes on wheels. They rode in their homes all day and then slept in them at night.
   Hint: The following steps require a lot of adult help.

2. Cut one of the wide sides off the refrigerator box.

3. Place the refrigerator box on its remaining long side, and cut several small windows in both short sides (while this is not historically accurate, it lets you see out while maintaining the box strength).

4. Use the utility knife (adult only) to cut the plastic hula hoops in half.

5. Securely tape the hoop halves to the top of the refrigerator box so that they arch over the box.

6. Drape the canvas fabric or blanket over the hoops to create the covered wagon top. Tape the fabric to keep it in place, if necessary.

7. Create four wood-look wheels by drawing them on the construction paper. Cut out the wheels and attach them to the sides of the refrigerator box wagon.

8. Prop the hobby horse up in front of the covered wagon.

9. Create a set of reins from the horses to the wagon with the sturdy rope.

10. If you like, put small boxes, old pots and pans, and tin cups in the wagon.

11. Dress up like a pioneer, and hit the trail!

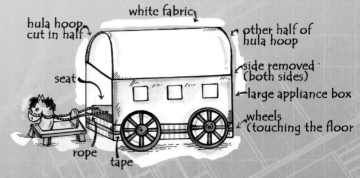

hula hoop cut in half

white fabric

other half of hula hoop

side removed (both sides)

large appliance box

wheels (touching the floor

seat

rope

tape

Puppet Theater

The show's the thing! Build your own puppet theater, and put on plays for your family and friends.

What You'll Need

construction paper

crayons

glue

large cardboard box, such as a refrigerator or appliance box

old sheet or large piece of cloth

scissors

utility knife (adult only)

wide masking or duct tape

Books to Enjoy

Jeremy and the Enchanted Theater by Becky Citra

Out and About at the Theater by Bitsy Kemper

The Unlikely Princess by Elizabeth Goodwin

What to do

1. Ask an adult to cut a window in one side of the box, removing the upper half of that side. Leave the top and other three sides intact.
2. Ask the adult to cut a door on the opposite side nearest the floor. The door should be large enough for you to crawl through easily.
3. With the tape, hang the sheet or fabric from the inside of the top of the box, in front of the window. This creates your puppet stage. (You may need an adult to help you with this step.)
4. Decorate the outside of your theater in any way you choose: color pictures on it, or cut out shapes from the construction paper to glue onto your theater. Make a sign for your theater, and glue it on the front.
5. Use your theater to put on a puppet show for your friends and family.

Index

General Index